Praise for *The*

In *The Riddle of Yes*, Carolyn Locke's luminous, meditative poems guide us on the one journey we all take. We experience the deaths of others and sense the steely presence of our own.

—Margaret Yocom, author of **ALL KINDS OF FUR**

Carolyn Locke's poems possess lyric qualities and move like a film of words.

—Joseph Zaccardi, Poet Laureate of Marin County, California (2013–2015) and author of four books of poetry, most recently *A Wolf Stands Alone in Water*

The poems in *The Riddle of Yes* by Carolyn Locke are not observations, thoughts, or reflections; they're direct experience.

—Barbaria Maria, author of *Crossing Time* and *Palace Boulevard*

Praise for *Always This Falling*

In *Always This Falling*, Carolyn Locke trains her clear gaze at the earth and the body: muscle and flesh, flower and root. Her questing spirit interrogates everything, unearthing the rich life beneath what we can see and taste. She celebrates our seasons of abundance and loss— what we risk and what we reap. Above all, these lucid, truthful poems shine with love.

—Joan Larkin author of *Blue Hanuman, My Body: New and Selected Poems, Cold River, A Long Sound,* and *Housework*

Praise for *Not One Thing: Following Matsuo Basho's Narrow Road to the Interior*

꩜

In a beautifully woven mix of poetry, prose, and photographs, Carolyn Locke shares a "diary of her heart," a record of a journey through northern Japan following in the footsteps of the haiku poet Basho and the waka poet Saigyo, who traveled before him. As she and her companions walk the paths generations of Japanese poets walked, she realizes that "wandering is like dance" and that what each contributes becomes part of "the choreography of our shared journey." *Not One Thing* welcomes readers into the dance with vivid description and haunting poetry and encourages them to contribute their own choreography as they travel along in imagination.

—Laurel Rasplica Rodd, Professor of Japanese and author of *Nichiren: A Biography* and *Kokinshu: A Collection of Poems Ancient and Modern*

Praise for *The Place We Become*

꩜

The Place We Become is indeed all about becoming. In Carolyn Locke's poems, transformation can occur through travel to foreign places—those "brief migrations into the world of the other"—or by deep attention to the sacredness of the natural world, where an overnight rainfall becomes "a torrential blessing we've forgotten to pray for." Locke's poems trace the process by which people slip identity and ego and enter into a larger space. She doesn't ignore what's broken, but balances it with images of a greater whole. These are poems that carry much wisdom and beauty.

—Betsy Sholl, Maine Poet Laureate (2006–2011) and author of eight collections of poetry, most recently, *Otherwise Unseeable* and *House of Sparrows: New and Selected Poems*

The
Riddle
of Yes

Poems by
CAROLYN LOCKE

for my sisters Ann and Sylvia
and sisters of the heart
LL, SG, DLE, VP

Table of Contents

How It Happens 3

Part One 5

In Her Skin 7
Premonition 8
Held by What She Isn't 10
Lament 11
In the Weave 12
What You Want 13
The Music of Stones 14
between friends 15
What's Missing 18
An Encounter 19
here, now 20
nothing else 21
Confusion in the Forest 22
Rufous-sided Towhee 23
Winter's Stream 24
this morning 25
For the Hiker Lost in Acadia 26
What Will We 28
One Song 29
Reluctance Before Spring 30
In the Pond 31
Swimming with My Father 32
In the Time of Trillium 33
In the Turning 34
returning 35
Today 36
If You Should Ask 37

Part Two...39

Buddha Bird 41
As If 42
In the Dark Hours 43
At Barred Island 44
Body Musings 45
When I Die 47
eclipse.. 48
On Composing a Death Poem 49
after the electrocution 50
The Party.. 51
Room One in the House of She......................52
i will...53
Room Two in the House of She......................54
Conundrum..55
Room Three in the House of She....................56
The Bell 57
Beginning, Again 58
The Gift..59
The Truth About Wings 60
Wanting to See 62
Of Time and the Wind 63
She Considers Protest.................................65
In the Well... 66
Bridging Suspension 67
she arrives in mexico 68
No Turning Back..69
She Becomes a Cathedral............................ 70
Rest in the Riddle of Yes 71

Acknowlegments 81
About the Author 85

How It Happens

She's different every day.
This morning, she's the sparrow
you half glimpse
in the hedgerow.

You try not to startle her,
take quiet, gentle steps.
Still, just when you think
you're close enough

to truly see her,
she flits ahead, slips
into leaf shadow
just beyond reach.

And it's not even
that you want
to hold her in your grasp,
that you need

to stroke the soft feathers
on her back, or feel
her warm heart beating.
You only want her

to stop long enough
for your eyes to meet,
for just one of hers
to look deep into yours,

and maybe, as you turn
and walk away, to carry
into the dark the song
she alone can sing.

Part One

In Her Skin

The whole time she's lived here, the river
has flowed in fog so dense she believed
there were no banks to contain it.

From time to time, silent as a cloud
gliding over the moon, a solitary skiff
passed by and vanished.

And all the while, time was suspended,
the way breath leaves the body,
hangs in the air on a cold winter morning.

Premonition
for Tanya

Geese are flying
      through my dreams,
            first a long, trailing V,

then a swirling circle
      of gabbling and honking
            spiraling in on itself

to a tight, pulsing orb.
            Something precious
                  I sense

is being held
      at the center—
            but before

I can grasp a thought
      beyond feeling,
            a lone goose

breaks free
      and drops to the ground.
            She stands before me,

shapeshifting—
      now a red fox
            with black-tipped ears.

Her golden eyes
      gaze into mine
            for one brief moment.

Then she turns,
      disappears into the woods,
                and I wake

to the emptiness
      of your leaving
            before you have gone.

Held by What She Isn't

She's been so patient, waiting on the corner
for something to happen. For someone

to tell her a secret or to hear
the secret she wants but doesn't want

to tell. She watches the light turn red, yellow,
green...red, yellow, green...unwilling to cross.

On the other side, sorrow is a blue-black robe
swaying in the trees. But isn't that what she wants?

Doesn't she long for something to balance
the oppressive light into which she's fallen?

Something to lessen the throat-aching
silence that keeps her here.

Lament

for Tanya

Each night I think of you
awake and alone,
listening to the sound
of your own heart beating—

how long? how long?
echoing deep in your bones
where the cancer grows.

Think of you
clutching in your fists
all you've been or loved,
pressing hard against your chest—

how long? how long?

In the Weave

She wants to go back, but the path has closed in behind her.
Roots and stones worn smooth by generations
are now covered in a cushion of moss, thick and virginal.
And a profusion of vines has snaked through the brush,
formed an impenetrable weave just inches above it.
To return she'd have to slither on her belly.

They call places like this hells, and in hells of this kind,
there is no light. But isn't all light relative? Maybe
if she waits long enough, she'll be able to see.
Still, there's the reality of the body itself to consider,
and whether space, too, is relative, whether what seems
impassable is actually so.

Perhaps it's only a matter of adjusting—
eyes to darkness, body to smaller and smaller spaces.

She hesitates, turns to look at the path ahead,
sees that it, too, has closed in, as dark and tight
as what's behind. Is there any point in moving?
No, she'll wait, wait for the light which will surely come.

What You Want

August brings a haunting quiet,
the earth holding its breath.

Oblivious to the tinge of sadness
in the slanting light
crickets chant endlessly.

You want to find
a sustaining miracle.

But caught between the desire
to lay yourself open
to whatever warmth remains

and the urge to curl inward
it's hard to know where to look.

Everything's shifting again.
All around you
lives are falling apart.

Sometimes it's easy to pretend
You'll go on like this forever,
and so you do—go on, I mean.

The Music of Stones

Morning sunlight awakens her body
to a hunger for something beyond itself.

In her hand she cradles two stones,
rubs each one firmly, hoping to release

the essence of island in Newfoundland's
glossy black, Iona's rough-hewn heart.

She knows little of stones,
but she'll play them until they sing

a melody of far-flung light
traveling through the wilderness.

between friends

for Tanya

1

the respirator breathes for you
in this shadowed room
and i hold your hand
feel beneath the skin
the bones of your fingers
gripping mine perhaps too late
i tell you i believe in death
we dissolve into something
greater than ourselves

2

you show me the stitches in your side
healing you say but oh the swelling
in your feet and ankles the slow wasting
away of muscles in your arms and legs
while each morning i lie on my back
lift legs toward the ceiling grip my ankles
stare at muscles still sculpted and healthy

3

the PET scan reveals tumors shrinking
maybe even disappearing
and you sit in your home
windows lit by candles
light snow falling as you sip kahlúa
wrap gift after gift as if you know
but refuse to believe
this christmas will be your last
can't imagine
how your appetite will shrivel
nor how cold you will be
even on the hottest days of summer

4

one morning you tell me
the straps of your prosthetic bra
are cutting into the thin flesh
of your shoulders you need help

and so like giddy teenagers we shop
for something different
sports bra too flat gel inserts too heavy
we discuss the pros and cons
of kleenex for stuffing can't stop
laughing in the face of this dilemma

5

do you think i will ever get better?
you ask *i want to be touched* you say
so tenuous this old and practiced dance
between what can be said
and what can't

6

you are miles away and yet
i feel you letting go watch
numbers on the clock advance
hear the phone ringing
then long overdue
the soft patter of rain on the roof
so many unanswered questions
unwinding through the universe

What's Missing

Heavy winds are churning
the steel sky above the river,
bringing with them the familiar
warmth of my mother's hands,
the kindness in my father's eyes.

I never knew loss
could be so deep, so absolute,
that I would always feel their presence
the way an amputee
still feels cold in a missing limb.

And that's another thing: the way
one ache leads to another, how
these naked trees make me long
for my children, for their growing
bodies once harbored within me.

As the winds die down, I turn
away from the water, breathe in
the faint scent of fallen apples.
Cold comes down sudden
and hard in the waning light.

An Encounter

In these woods the scent of decaying leaves
fills her. Where the path curves away
from the stone wall, a figure in a long hooded cape
stands facing her. Without hesitation she moves

toward it, the face and frame of white hair
coming into sharper focus with every step.
Eyes the color of lapis, lips offering just a hint
of smile. The figure raises her hand, beckons,

then turns and slowly walks away.
A few paces behind, she follows her
through the late afternoon. Light and shadow
breathe across the forest floor.

At the edge of a still pond, they stop to watch
the full moon rise behind slender trunks of birches
on the far shore and climb through a lacework
of branches. A pair of white cranes goes unnoticed

until they begin to dance, lifting first one foot,
then the other in and out of the water, opening
and closing their wings, circling and bowing.
Their quiet jabbering echoes across the water.

She moves to stand close to the old woman.
They reach out, clasping hands, and tremble
as a sudden whoosh of wings lifts the cranes
over the treetops and into the darkening sky.

here, now

outside, all is rust and gray and muted green
while in this room the singing bowl stretches
her to a fine line that slips under the windowsill
disappears over the horizon sways and swirls
lengthens and contracts widens and thins in
the strangeness of being

nothing else

press *play* and the chant of the Dalai Lama
fills the room   as if he knows who you are

the grace of sound as it travels
the distance to silence   the moon wanes

and winter waits on its haunches   clarity
just out of reach   white wilderness

curve of the earth   beyond which emptiness
exists   the body translucent among memories

so hard to leave the silence   words
now irrelevant   the mind unable to snatch meaning

from being   pull of breath
as it moves   through the body

Confusion in the Forest

It starts when she looks in the mirror
and isn't there. All she sees

is the reflection of an open window
leading to a flowered field.

What else can she do
but climb out, or maybe into?

And when she looks back,
the mirror is gone,

the field and window, too,
and she's in a forest,

heavy snow falling,
no footsteps to follow.

It's frightening, really—
everyone else so sure

while she stands alone and bewildered,
snow piling up fast around her.

Rufous-sided Towhee

One morning she wakes with a bird in her belly,
feels its flutterings, sees clearly the sooty black
chest, head, and back, ivory spots on the wings,
luminous red-brown sides, startling white stomach.

How she knows it's injured, she can't say,
nor how it has settled inside her. Certainly
it's not up to her to care for it. She refuses
to name it, goes on with her day as if

it isn't there, hoping it will disappear
as suddenly as it arrived.
But with twilight's first flicker
comes a plaintive song, threading

through the tangled thicket of her body,
rippling in her bloodstream, and she knows
it must belong to her. She will be obliged
to hold it through the wingless night.

Winter's Stream

She won't always be sitting here, but for now
it's what she wants—this lacework of ice
growing closer and closer to the dark center
with each cold night, the riveting black and white
keeping her still. She knows she's not alone.

High in the hemlock two porcupines
are sleeping, one on the far end of the branch,
the other nestled beside the trunk. They seem not
to have moved for days although the branches
littering the snow beneath the tree tell another story.

Somewhere in the brush, the snowshoe hare
must be watching, her nose twitching. And, too,
the trail is pockmarked with hoofprints of deer
meandering off into the woods, then returning.
And at night there is no denying the barred owl

who calls from a distant and nameless place.

this morning

snowflakes drift
    on gray silence

metal-cold moon
    just a memory

whatever clarity
    you thought

was yours
    balancing

on the blade
    of night

dissolves
    with this

day's sun
    inscrutable

behind a scrim
    of clouds

For the Hiker Lost in Acadia

Six days after you set foot on the path,
I look across Eagle Lake to Sargent Mountain
and all the hills between, try to imagine
what could've happened to you that day.

No doubt the wilderness called you,
as it called us today, into the bitter cold,
the biting wind, and thick gray clouds
promising snow by dark. No doubt

you believed in your own invincibility
as we all must if we're to keep going.
And so what was your undoing?
Ice on a steep slope? A fall

and a broken limb? Heart failure?
Or did you merely lose your way?
A last phone call from the mountaintop, then
silence as snow fell through the long night.

You disappeared without a trace.
I want to believe in your final hours
you had no regrets, want to believe
you were where you wanted—even

needed—to be, and that you came
to rest peacefully beneath the snow.
Far ahead on the trail and so small
against these mountains he loves,

my husband disappears in swirling snow.
With a catch in my throat, I tell myself
once more, *Everyone deserves to live
and die on his own terms.*

What Will We

The great maple in front of the house is down,
felled by a rogue gust of wind from the north.
Branches full of winter buds sprawl across the lawn,
and a spike of splintered trunk pokes at the sky.

We want nothing more than to cut it up and cart it away,
this fallen body pelted by ice and rain and snow—
want no reminders that we have been its final caretakers,
keepers of a covenant passed from generation to generation
to cultivate its summer shade, protect its autumn splendor.

For forty years we coddled, pruned and cabled branches,
and the tree held firm, filtering light and casting shadows
through our rooms in every season, patiently entwined
its music with ours. But today the house trembles

at the crunch of the chipper chewing branches,
and the whine of the chainsaw ripping through the trunk.
It quakes with each thunk of the ax splitting the core,
shudders at the heavy thud of collapse.

What will the house—
what will we—be without it?

One Song
for Gerry

Yesterday I pressed my ear against your chest
listening for the beat of that faithful muscle at
the center of you and me. And today?

Today we went in search of snowy owls
along mountain ridges
and in deep sunless ravines.

If they were there,
they kept to themselves, as did we,
hiking without words, our footsteps

falling in their practiced, syncopated
way. All around us winter sun
gilded waters of the bay,

silvered needles of hemlock and pine
while an iron weave of roots
held firm beneath us.

Reluctance Before Spring

Lately, the deer have been stepping out of snowy woods
and onto the roads. In early morning on my way to work,
a trio cavort in front of me, and on Route 1 another leaps
out of darkness into the beam of my headlights. Then one,
two, three, four come bounding across Route 7 at twilight.
I slam on the brakes. In seconds I'm at a dead halt.

No collision, no crumpled car, no shattered windshield—
only a drumming in my chest pleading for the green world
to unfold. Yet in the silent aftermath, a softness in my belly,
a yearning for dark shadows playing over white,
for the openness of leafless trees. I am not ready

to be pushed out of quiet darkness into a world
about to explode—wood frogs and peepers charging
the air with their collective chant, leaves expanding
into a thousand shades of green, bird song
without end. I emerge blinking in the light, feel a perverse
uneasiness at earth's slow tilting toward the gaudy sun.

In the Pond

At dusk, she finds the water flat. Then
a sudden breeze ripples the surface.

Colors shift—slate blue to cream,
then inky gray. Lace of green algae

spreads across the rocky shore.
She's been waiting for memories

to speak, but it seems they've all drifted
to the bottom and closed their mouths.

She follows them down, looks up
through the water. One by one, stars emerge.

She wills them to sink, to lie beside her
and make soundless memories sing.

Swimming with My Father

I'd stand on the shore and watch him
walk into the water. When it reached
the lower edge of his red trunks, he'd stop,
wet his arms, splash his chest, then move
farther out. Waist deep, he'd scoop water
in his hands, christen his face, plunge head
first. I couldn't wait for him
to come up laughing and turn toward me.

He'd swim back and carry me out
to where my toes could not touch bottom,
rest me belly down on the water's surface,
and with the lightest touch of his palm
keep me lifted as I kicked my feet,
spouting fountains high in the air.

In the Time of Trillium

for my mother

When the trees are filled with robins singing
and the swamp with chanting peepers,
when days are a lime-green glow
and small suns of daffodils explode
at the edge of the woods, when garden tulips
swell with pink and red and orange possibility,
and tiny black buds of lilac promise abundance,
once again I see your body releasing you
into the blue-black night where Venus hangs
like a jewel above thickening grasses.

In the Turning

She wakes to gray-blue silence,
her small canoe drifting in the current.

On the water, almost imperceptible,
the wake of an old companion,

perhaps making for home. From here
the coastline is a shadowed haze,

nothing on which to hang memory,
nothing leading her forward.

For such a long time she's forgotten
about the paddle, its polished handle

resting against the gunwale, and the way
it felt to hold it in her hands.

This, she knows, is the only way back—
to paddle closer and closer to shore,

examine each boulder, each curve of land,
each hill, until something says, *Land here.*

returning

i am standing   at the living room window
small hands gripping the sill   looking out
into branches of the fir   home
to the robin's nest   three downy heads
open beaks   waiting to be fed

i let go of the sill   step backward
one   two   three   four
each step   more wobbly than the last
i crouch   lean forward   place hands
and knees   on the floor   crawl backward
knee then hand   then knee then hand
until toes   touch my mother's feet

i push myself up   sit on my bottom
raise my arms   and feel her hands
around my ribs   lifting me to her lap
her arms   enfolding me

i close my eyes   return to darkness
two hearts   beating in unison
my mother's blood   pulsing through me

i follow its flow to a sourceless source
every living thing   a rose reversing itself
petals fold   become a seed within a seed

my face is a seed in the wind   is the emptiness
between   is the wind

Today

nothing
whispers of the past—

not a spider's footprint
on the page, not

the smooth black stone
beside the ticking clock,

not the warbler
trilling in the hedgerow—

even the turtle
who waited so long

beneath the ice
has forgotten the map

of light she followed
to this log, her old shell

gleaming in the sun
as if everything from before

has vanished into the fullness
of this impossible green.

If You Should Ask

If you should ask her where she's been all this time,
she would say somewhere in thick meadow grass
where the wind shuffles its feet; down by the sea,
she would say, trying to unravel the mystery of water,
its ebb and flow, trickle, gush, babble to stillness;
she would say she's been to the top of the tallest pine
where the sky begins; in the stars, she would say,
looking down on boats that travel the river's spine,
and in this body that lives at once in this
and every moment, every place it's ever been.

Part Two

Buddha Bird

This morning we were watching a cardinal sitting on the bare ground of the walkway, speculating on why it didn't move. "How strange," we said. "Birds never do that." And then I said, "I wonder if he's okay?" "Of course he is," you said. "Probably he just likes feeling the bare ground on his feet." But I began to worry. "Look at that! Something just spooked the mourning doves and they've all flown into the trees, but he hasn't moved at all! Has he even turned his head?" "I think so," you said. "Oh, that's good," I said, and took another sip of coffee. "I'll bet he's meditating," I mused. "Yes, he's a Buddha bird," I said with conviction. All through breakfast, we watched and waited for something to happen. And yes I *know* a watched pot never boils, but sometimes you *have* to do it—watch, I mean—even when you know it won't make any difference. But don't get me started on all the things that need watching these days—rips in the cheesecloth of this country opening up like chasms in every direction, and how can we keep our eyes on every one of them? But if we don't, we're liable to find ourselves without a cloth to stand on, cover us, hold us together, or whatever the fabric of society does. But that's just it, see? We were watching this morning, our eyes on that bird—not even blinking—only to discover that what we thought we were watching wasn't a bird at all, but a red leaf resting against the shrinking snow bank. So that's how it is—you think you're focused, paying attention, keeping your eye on the ball, but it isn't even a ball you're watching.

As If

No one knows what happened in the water,
only that it was found on the beach
at 11:30 a.m., an unidentified female body.

It must be the suddenness that shakes us,
those unexpected final moments
we can't imagine—
will the water be cold or warm?
will a cramp pull us down,
or muscles simply fail
against a strong current?
what final image
will flicker in the mind
before we sink into darkness?

And so again and again
we tell the story as if it were ours—
the report on the news,
the husband watching,
unable to believe
the body might be hers.

In the Dark Hours

Step into the stillness of this stone. Find
where it has lain beside the sea or under,
uncountable years of sun and stars.

In its faint grooves feel the echo
of feather, fin, leaf, blade of grass,
or shell cast upon its surface.

Hold it in your palm just so,
your fingers curling around it.
Think of bodies, their boundaries

and secret places, what ancient energy
they hold and release. Sit in this stone
and hear what you hear—

lightning crack of ice, whistling wings,
rumble in the valley,
human voices calling from the desert.

At Barred Island

Moan of the whistle buoy
       penetrates muscle and bone.
            Two halves of the sea

surge toward the bar
       that joins land to land—
            east flowing west,

west flowing east—
       until waters touch,
            mingle, become one

in their insistence
       to separate earth
            from earth, to create

an island
       that will be island
            only as long

as these waters rise
       and hold. Here the osprey
            and I have chosen

to nest, crying out
       to the eternal tides
            I am! I am!

Body Musings

Awakening

Sparkling light uncurls the body,
stretches it, hands palm to palm,
into a vast emptiness.

The Big Toe Speaks

Shaped like the toe of your father,
I am the base of your Self—
touchstone to earth and balance.

Note to My Daughter

Haunted by the soft edges
of your childhood paintings,
pastel forms floating in bubbles,

I feel you still

swimming within me
in the time
before you were you.

Fear's Articulation

Lately, at every solstice, muscles
just beneath the shoulder blades
tighten their grip in endless
contractions, hold fear hostage.

But once, in a moment of inattention,
the back's fist opened

and a voice spoke:

Do not abandon
long hours of darkness
for those of light
nor mistake one for the other.

Abide with each in equal measure.

What you will find is a cove
emptying and filling without end.

When I Die

scatter my ashes
      on ocean waters
            let waves rock me

until I dissolve
      into nothing
         and everything

let me find my way
      to Orion Nebula
         to light glinting

in the open palm
      of the scallop shell
         let the whistle buoy

sound the days
      of my passing
           sea glass

hold the years of my living

eclipse

her body curled like a fetus
she waits
beside an open window

hears only the faint
rustle of leaves
a dog barking in the distance

crossbeams of light
emanate from the moon
probing deep within her

and heart cells quicken
as earth's shadow creeps
across its bone-white face

just before total darkness
a slim golden crescent
rims its outer edge

then disappears and she feels
the moon pulsing ruby red
while all around it

glittering stars explode
drawing her back
to that celestial sea

original and infinite breath

On Composing a Death Poem
for my children

Here on the far edge of the island
looking out to sea, I tell you,
is where I want my end to be.

Write it down, you say, and I say
I have. But now the cottage
is emptied of you, and I'm held hostage

by the irrational fear of losing
before the loss—oh how
will I ever float away and leave you?

after the electrocution

life begins the eternity of the body electrified every cell tingling every sense jarred beyond recognition church bells echoing ever and forever full-bodied wine and a charbroiled steak last supper on your tongue and against your skin warm water flowing scent of lavender final cleansing filling you with wonder and the sky ablaze with never-ending light you an infinite explosion reverberating through the universe after the electrocution boredom is impossible so go ahead execute if you must

The Party

She could stop talking before it's too late, but words keep tumbling out of her mouth—meaningless, disconnected, empty. Parties. She loathes parties. The way she always ends up in a conversation that peters out, and here she is again, trapped in a space with someone she hardly knows, unable to set herself free without being rude. She hates the way her own eyes and those of the one facing her scan the room looking for a way out, focus on the dish of cashews just out of reach, move on to the wine bottles on the counter, then back to the empty glass in her hand, the way bits of conversations in the corners of the room and across the table amplify the potential for silence between herself and the other. No, she can't let it happen, and so she keeps talking on and on when all she wants is to stop, become invisible, slip out to the porch where she can stare at the stars and breathe. Instead, she feels herself splinter into pieces too small to be recovered and fall to the floor. Now, whoever she's been talking to is looking down at what's left of her, open-mouthed and stupefied.

Room One in the House of She

Before she entered this room, she thought
she was herself, but now she's stepped inside

and she isn't. Held in a block of ice
she peers through translucent walls—

the vase impossible to distinguish
from the burgundy roses it holds, oak table

slowly melting into emerald
and indigo swirls in the rug.

Silence is a black stone expanding.
She tilts her head, desperate to hear something—

the strains of a Brahms concerto, or even
just the steady tick of a clock on the wall.

Nothing. She presses her spine against the ice,
slides to the floor, rests her head on raised knees.

i will

my brother's death is crushing water pressing me deep and deeper still unable to catch my breath every now and then a glimmer from above pulling me up and out of it the glaring light too much to bear and i'm going down again gulping water saving hands plunging after but all i want is the mesmerizing drumbeat against my chest to stop *mea culpa mea culpa* hear oh hear the sin that is mine and for which i will never be forgiven will never confess i defy you to love me and if you even try i will take you down with me

Room Two in the House of She

Confined as she is to the next room,
she looks for what lies beneath the surface.

An old cord—rotted, grimy, secretive—
rests on the table beside the brown couch.

Brighter than any she's ever known,
the bare lightbulb above offers no help.

A harp stares at her from the corner,
its mouth full of silent strings reproaching her

for something she's done or forgotten to do—
she doesn't know which—and a knot in the floor

is saying the same thing. And so it's difficult
not to think of sledgehammers,

the walls of her shame crumbling
and rising in a fine gray dust.

Conundrum

Placing each foot with care, she walks slowly in early morning,
thinks today she will do no harm. Meanwhile, with every step

she crushes tender blades of grass, white clover blossoms,
fronds of plants she can't name. She comes upon a city of ants,

little pyramids nestled in the grass, uncountable tiny bodies
crawling in and out, up, down, and around, going about

their business in the sudden shadow of her enormous presence.
A thrush sings in the woods. An echo replies. Again she thinks,

I will do no harm, all the while trampling on what has waited
all winter in the frozen ground to live. She lifts her foot,

sees them bounce back—the green grass, the moss, the clover—
but those clever ant hills? No. Those inside who have survived

the carnage must tunnel up to the surface, begin again
amid scattered corpses. Like the dolphins and the whales,

the monkeys and so many others, do they mourn their dead?
Do no harm, no harm, she whispers.

Room Three in the House of She

Outside, a storm tosses the trees, rain
batters the house, thunder strides the sky.

She sits cross-legged in the center
of an ivory room where a crystal cube

on the pine floor casts iridescent lavender
and tangerine on the walls. A weathered

ladder, almost touching the ceiling,
is balanced precariously against it.

A tiny porcelain horse the color of mint
looks down from a shelf,

and beside it, lilacs in a cobalt vase
fill the air with a sacred scent.

The Bell

She never said she believes in it,
but when the bell rings out
across the star-filled sky, she knows

she must leave her house,
walk down dark streets
to the town center.

The clanging is so loud
she covers her ears, and
when she steps onto the green,

she begins pressing palms to ears
hard against the sound,
then gently lifting them away—

pressing and lifting, pressing
and lifting—until the ringing
enters her belly, expands

and contracts with every breath,
and she
is inside the bell swinging

back and forth, striking against
its metal skin
until she knows nothing else.

Beginning, Again

Just before the door slams shut,
she turns back, catches a glimpse
of blue gauze floating across the room.

Was the window open? A breeze
coming through? What else
has she missed in her haste to depart?

But that door will never open again,
and the house is lost to her.
Still, she has the garden, a place

not haunted by ghosts or gauze,
where she can bathe
in the sweet scent of nicotiana.

The Gift

Inside the nest of green tissue paper
is a hand-carved yellow warbler,
each feather precisely hewn and glowing,
each wing just beginning
to lift away from the body.

She strokes with her finger, working
down one side of the spine,
then the other, to the tip
of tail feathers, over and over,

until she's finally able
to free the bird from its box,
rest it on her outstretched palm,
begin to explore the space
behind its inscrutable black eye.

The Truth About Wings

We are only just now beginning to look...
she hears them say. The rest is lost
in the haze rising between her and them
as her eyes grow cloudy and her ears plugged.

She has no idea what they're looking for,
but it doesn't matter. She's too busy
adjusting to the growth of wings fanning out
from her shoulders, worrying about how
she'll navigate the world without seeing
or hearing, wondering what she'll learn.

If she flaps these wings will they lift her
off the ground? And if so, then what?

And so it's easy to understand how quickly
she forgets about the others, concentrates
only on touch and smell
to find the thin line between one thing
and another. As for them, if they were still
searching, they wouldn't find her.

Later, against all odds, she appears
somewhere else. Cold moisture seeps
through her skin, but even now she can't
see or hear anything. She's been flying,
hasn't she? At least the wind
streaming over her body made her think so.

Now the scent of salt and sweetgrass
fills her nostrils. Is she somewhere in
the marshes at the edge of the sea?

Those who come upon her haven't been
looking for her, and first impressions are less
than promising. She lies prone in the mud,
her once dazzling wings frayed and protruding
from her body at awkward angles.

Startled by hands cupping her head and sliding
beneath her body, she senses she's being lifted
and carried some distance, then placed down gently,
her cheek pressed against soft sand.

The air turns chill and she shudders
with stark recognition that she's once again
grounded and alone. Yet every body part
is still breathing, cajoling, *Let be...let be...*
soon enough you will melt into the earth that holds you.
You will have no need of wings. Let be...

Wanting to See

Now she finds herself among the thousands—
hunch-backed, curled inward, shoulders up
around their ears, eyes darting from side to side,
flinching at every unexpected sound.

Yes, she, too, is clasping and wringing her hands,
scurrying for dark corners, not wanting to be seen,
not wanting to see. But when she closes her eyes,
a line of figures draped in lavender appears.

Each one holding an unquenchable flame,
they wind through the streets of cities, towns,
and villages, penetrate forests, circle ponds
and lakes, climb mountains, descend
into valleys. Following rivers to the sea,
they step onto all manner of floating craft,
ride the tides to the horizon. And they rise up
into the sky, come down in falling rain.

These she holds close to her heart, which aches
with a sadness beyond words, until they enter
her blood and glow in every breath.
Only then does she open her eyes and see
she can stand tall, shoulders back,
and walk into what seems like endless night,
the fire at her core flaring out into the darkness.

Of Time and the Wind

These days, time is holding her,
inviting her to be in it, with it,

carried by it on endless waves
that never find a shore

on which to break. These days
she's breathing,

watching the eye of time
watching her.

And on this morning, she feels
the presence of the wind

brushing each newborn leaf
on maple, aspen, oak, and pin cherry,

sees how it passes
through grass and ferns,

swirls around sudden blossoms
of honeysuckle and dogwood,

slips between the startling
pale tips of fir and hemlock.

And in the stand of ash,
for the first time, she hears

the quiet clacking
of one branch against another.

She Considers Protest

Once she thought she could join the cacophony,
be another loud voice, but now she's heard chimes
in the distant mountains, the tapping of metal
against metal in the wind. And when she remembers

the voices, all that emotion released
in high-pitched squeals, the screech of tension
simultaneously battering and draining her,
she knows she can no longer endure them.

No, she needs to find the high mountain places,
move closer to the thin crescent moon, feel it
waxing and waning, as her own face darkens
day by day and her body empties, becomes
an instrument of the wind—an offering of sorts.

In the Well

She peers through the darkness
into a faceless reflection at the bottom,

searches for eyes, mouth, anything familiar,
but there's only a motionless gray oval.

She watches for a long time, thinking
something will change—her eyes

will adjust and focus, an image
become visible. The quiet is immense.

In slow circular motions, she strokes
her cheeks, palpates the bones

around eye sockets, slides a finger down
the length of her nose, outlines her lips.

Resting elbows on the edge, cupping
her chin in her hands, she scrutinizes

the distant oval. It remains expressionless,
offers only the surprise of blessed stillness.

Bridging Suspension

She's a cartoon on a dead run
suddenly stopped
beyond the cliff's edge

ignoring the void beneath her.
Her eyes are level with the setting sun.
Perseverance has brought her here

and she isn't about to plummet now.
With each intake of breath,
she expands, becomes lighter

yet more substantial as she floats
toward gold bleeding into scarlet,
deep purple, and mauve.

she arrives in mexico

where she is an echo of every where and every time and always who she was is will be is the red winter house conversing with old ghosts the blizzard swirling around it and the body traveling from darkness to darkness is the sunrise about to bloom a sudden explosion of azure and orange and rose and turquoise is the music of a heartbeat on steroids and the weight of the glittering sun dropping into the pacific is the bus hugging the coastline crawling uphill snaking around corners screaming down the other side is light to light a dazzling glow and the tropical heat that cradles her is the clicking gecko the pounding surf the cricket creaking in the walkway is the sliver of moon in the blue hour the new language she hears but cannot speak is the taste of chili jalapeños and coconuts

No Turning Back

She's left early, not believing that once the sun has set,
there could be anything more dazzling than that orb
in the western sky. But now she sees the canyon walls

vermillion and glowing from within. She's heard
of people who stride through flames unscathed,
decides this is a fire she needs to test.

First tentative, then determined, she closes her eyes,
extends her arms, palms facing forward, and navigates
by the heat. The burning sinks into her skin,

probes deeper, almost searing the muscles beneath.
A step closer and the line between the fierce light
around her and the darkness within slowly dissolves.

She Becomes a Cathedral

Of course she's seen their windows before, been mesmerized
by light penetrating ruby, emerald, lapis, and gold,
by the way it falls transformed on pew, pulpit, or stone floor.

But never has she seen such a window
as when she looks in the mirror and opens her mouth.
There at the back of her throat, three transparent panes
arc upward and narrow to a single point.

And the searing white light that blazes through the glass
is rising out of a black sky within her
rife with the thrum of stars.

Rest in the Riddle of Yes

There's no secret ingredient—what comes to her comes, and she lives
without precision, reaching for what should come next and following.
First, her skin melts and then one by one each layer below, until
she's only bones radiating light. And so, it's imperative that she leave.

She walks out into the world, a breeze circling her joints, weaving
through her rib cage, the sun sinking deep into marrow. At dusk,
all color draining from the sky, she sees at the edge of the field, a circle
of hunched forms shrouded in gray. She doesn't sleep but watches.

Whether they sleep during the night she can't tell. They never move
but fade in and out of the fog that swells with dawn. Crows come
circling in silence overhead, wings flapping through heavy air.
Slowly they unwind themselves and fly in a line toward the river,

lead her to this bank where the water is whispering, *Hush...hush...*
there's music to be found here. She's ready now to enter the stream,
water flowing over her, morning light dappling through waves, ready
to lie with the stones beneath her. Bones of the body, bones of the earth.

Acknowledgments

A sincere thank you to the editors of the following publications in which these poems first appeared, sometimes in different versions:

Aurorean: "Today"

Cafe Review: "For the Hiker Lost in Acadia" and "Reluctance Before Spring"

Calyx: "She Becomes a Cathedral"

Clockhouse: "Rest in the Riddle of Yes"

Connecticut River Review: "In the Time of Trillium"

Earth's Daughters: "Winter's Stream"

Goose River Anthology: "eclipse," "The Music of Stones" (formerly entitled "In Two Worlds"), "What's Missing," and "Premonition"

Pudding Magazine: "What Will We," "Swimming with My Father," and "In the Turning"

Sun Journal: "How It Happens"

Third Wednesday: "In the Dark Hours" and "In the Pond"

Acknowledgments *continued*

Heartfelt thanks to those who read and encouraged this manuscript: Kathleen Ellis, Sheila Gilluly, Ellen Goldsmith, Linda Lord, Barbaria Maria, Diane Green-Minor, Victoria Pittman, Sandy Weisman, and Chrystal Wing. Thanks also to the members of Barbaria's Belfast writing group (Jennifer Armstrong, Meredith Bruskin, Betsy Headley, Kathryn Robyn, Elizabeth Schaab, and Karin Spitfire) for their camaraderie and insightful comments on individual poems; to attendees of the Clockhouse Writers Conference and Retreat, where many of these poems began; and to Belfast Poet Laureate Tom Moore for selecting "What You Want," "In the Turning," and "Swimming with My Father" as part of his Poem of the Week project. And finally, much love and special thanks to Gerry, Jeff, and Alison, who are always there for me.

About the Author

CAROLYN LOCKE was born and grew up in Hudson, New Hampshire and has lived in Troy, Maine since 1974. A graduate of Bates College with a Bachelor of Arts in English and of Goddard College with a Master of Fine Arts in Creative Writing, she taught English and humanities for many years at the secondary level. She was a semifinalist for Maine Teacher of the Year and a recipient of a three-week Fulbright Memorial Fund trip to Japan, a six-week Fulbright-Hays Seminar in Morocco, two three-week Primary Source trips to China, and a four-week Fulbright-Hays Special Projects trip to Japan.

She has previously published two poetry collections—*Always This Falling* and *The Place We Become*—and the haibun *Not One Thing: Following Matsuo Basho's Narrow Road to the Interior*, which combines haiku, prose, and original photographs in a meditative journal about her travels in Japan. Her poems have appeared in numerous publications and the anthologies *Take Heart: Poems from Maine* edited by Maine Poet Laureate Wes McNair and *Poetry of Presence: An Anthology of Mindfulness Poems* edited by Phyllis Cole-Dai and Ruby Wilson. In addition, her poems have twice been cited in Maine Writers & Publishers Alliance competitions and selected for the *Poems from Here* radio series with Maine Poet Laureate Stuart Kestenbaum. She was a presenter at the Belfast Poetry Festival in 2011 and 2014, and she was the featured poet in 2015 at the 9th Annual Hugh Ogden Memorial Poetry Evening in Rangeley, Maine.